Ignite Life

Poetry Devotional

By Nurse Anne

Spill your passion to ignite

healing and blessings for all!

Intro:

"As you go" dare to inspire and bless everyone in your path.

The life stories we encounter daily are filled with struggle, triumph, joy, sorrow, self-doubt, and everything in between.

Challenge yourself to discover these stories and ignite passion and potential for your own journey along with mutual encouragement for others.

As a certified emergency and mental health registered nurse on the frontlines for over 30 years and still going, I am continually learning humanity on every level. Our individual experiences collide to weave a patchwork of beauty and grace.

Thanks:

To the memory of Tony: Brother, son, friend. Thanks for sharing your joy of soul and zeal for life. Truly a healing blessing for all!

Sons, JB and Jordan: Your diligence, creativity, love, and determination are my inspiration!

Mom and Dad: Thanks for your kindness, integrity, humor, help, and sharing of life!

Sister Danielle and family: Thanks for your genuine example, fun times shared, and immense life help!

Friends, readers, co-lifers. Be blessed and inspired!

2023 by Nurse Anne

Scripture from KJV version

Any examples or stories are purely coincidental and not taken from any persons specific life details.

Be inspired and renewed as you enjoy this labor of joy and love!

Contents:

1. Outward Mirror

2. Hide or Confide

3. Trapped in Memories

4. Single Parent

5. Street Survivors

6. Bondage

7. Battered

8. Inferior

9. Weary Travelers

10. Strangers

11. Limitations

12. Unique

13. Touch

14. Windows

15. Nature Love

16. Exotic Adventure

17. Family Time

18. Notice Me

19. Kindness

20. Generosity

21. Friends

22. Your Turn

Isaiah 43:19 KJV

Behold, I will do a new thing; now it shall spring forth; shall ye not know it? I will even make a way in the wilderness, and rivers in the desert.

1. Outward Mirror

Is it all about me?

OR

Can it be you, us, we?

The focus is real.

How do I choose?

Looking in my mirror.

OR

Centering on how YOU feel?

Is it always me, me, me indeed?

OR

Do I dare ask what YOU might need?

Every moment offers another choice.

Ruminate my inner feelings.

OR

Tune in to YOUR hearts voice.

Is it all about me?

OR

Can it be you, us, we?

In the practice of mindfulness, we are guided to notice everything in the moment, everything around us. Flowers, birds, trees, the sky, blades of grass, tiny insects, the voice of the wind, the sound of our feet walking on the gravel, water pouring from a faucet………..

Along with noticing nature, objects, and our own vibrations, we will also inspire encouragement and fortitude in the lives of others by providing personalized eye contact and attention to the details of someone's unique perspective and life journey. This outward focus will brighten the soul of others, along with sparking our own curiosity, learning, and empathy on our mutual worldwide adventures.

Philippians 2:2-4

2 Fulfil ye my joy, that ye be likeminded, having the same love, being of one accord, of one mind.

3 Let nothing be done through strife or vainglory; but in lowliness of mind let each esteem other better than themselves.

4 Look not every man on his own things, but every man also on the things of others.

2. Hide or Confide

Why all the sadness?

What's causing your tears?

Does your life seem like madness,

Filled with pain, sorrow, a host of all fears?

Would you allow me to peer on the inside?

Share just a fraction of your heart.

OR

Will your doubt cause you to run, cower, wanting to hide?

Take a small chance.

To show me the hurt.

Perhaps with some caring

I'll help you to dance.

When noticing someone that's quiet, seemingly enveloped in pain, sometimes we can be unsure of how to reach out. Therefore, we may also keep quiet for fear of saying the wrong thing.

But, conversely, when we do take that chance, and dare to discover what is burdening their soul, most of the time we encounter some sense of relief in the other because we would choose to care enough to ask anyway. Have you noticed that people experiencing grief, tragedy, and or generalized sadness are actually alright with sharing their story to someone who will take that time to listen?

Galatians 6:2

2 Bear ye one another's burdens, and so fulfil the law of Christ.

3. Trapped in Memories

The gray hair, wrinkling of skin, a vacant look in her eye.

No one who visits.

Isolated in my room.

Why am I just wishing for days gone by?

Lonely and bored.

Just sitting in this chair.

Staring out the window.

Why doesn't anyone care?

The staff is so busy.

I don't want to complain.

I'll just daydream in this place

While I watch outside all the rain.

If you find a spare moment

come sit by my bed.

Read me a story.

Even though, tears I might shed.

Our busy and scattered lives can leave some feeling lonely and abandoned. Some isolated souls are starved for companionship and conversation. Whether visiting a loved one or volunteering to reminisce with a person in need, this time well spent will be a blessing to all.

2 Corinthians 4:16

16 For which cause we faint not; but though our outward man perish, yet the inward man is renewed day by day.

Psalm 71:18

18 Now also when I am old and greyheaded, O God, forsake me not; until I have shewed thy strength unto this generation, and thy power to every one that is to come.

4. Single Parent

Mom is doing this alone

Always at work.

Kids have to reach her

only by phone.

The job, the chores.

No time to relax

Or even be bored.

Sometimes in this world.

It seems like the norm

We need others to assist.

To guide and to form.

Yes, I know it's not your job.

My kids are my own.

But I appreciate any help.

As I nurture my home.

Friends, family, neighbors, and after school programs can be a great blessing to help shape the lives of our future generation and provide support to overburdened caretakers. Thanks to all who undergo this endeavor in spite of your own busy lives.

Psalm 68:5

5 A father of the fatherless, and a judge of the widows, is God in his holy habitation.

5. Street Survivors

Cold dark concrete.

Stomach full of hunger.

How do I survive

Or warm my bare feet?

Danger and fears

Surround me like fog

The sun batters down

Advancing my years.

Is all this my fault?

Did I deserve the abuse?

My childhood was flawed.

I feel of no use.

Trauma-informed care implores us to look past the exterior and to quell our judgment. What has this person endured ? Do they have the tools to heal? Can we show compassion in action?

Isaiah 25:4

4 For thou hast been a strength to the poor, a strength to the needy in his distress, a refuge from the storm, a shadow from the heat, when the blast of the terrible ones is as a storm against the wall.

6. Bondage

Stolen from home.

Lured to a lie.

Now I'm trapped.

Might be better just to die.

Forced to this labor.

This disgust, feeling the shame.

Hoping for rescue.

Was tricked into this for fame.

Human trafficking invades every country, city, and neighborhood. People can be lured by deception for a myriad of reasons. Poverty, loneliness, trying to fit in, and many more reasons are used by perpetrators to capture their victims. We must educate, empower, and support organizations to eradicate this disgusting evil.

Psalm 82:3

3 Defend the poor and fatherless: do justice to the afflicted and needy.

Isaiah 1:17

17 Learn to do well; seek judgment, relieve the oppressed, judge the fatherless, plead for the widow.

7. Battered

Made to feel worthless.

Slapped for burnt dinner.

Always told she's a loser.

Lost her hope to ever be a winner.

Battered and bruised.

No strength to refute.

Accept the dark fate.

The lies, the trauma.

A life of being used.

Please help your sister.

Show her another way

Compassion and truth.

Hope for light of starting a new day.

Generational cycles, low self-esteem, and stressful surroundings can unfortunately perpetuate the pain of abuse.

Help us lead men, women and children to safer environments and promote trauma-informed care and learning to work on breaking the devastating cycles.

No one deserves to live in fear and torment.

2 Samuel 22:49

49 And that bringeth me forth from mine enemies: thou also hast lifted me up on high above them that rose up against me: thou hast delivered me from the violent man.

8. Inferior

Self-loathing – I don't measure up.

How will I compare?

Just want to fit in.

and stop wishing life was unfair.

My reflection seems subpar.

My size – my shape.

I don't dress like a star.

When will I be enough?

Satisfied with what I see

Content to be unique.

Let go and just be.

You are enough!

We do not have to fit into a certain mold or adopt the so-called cool way to fit in that is promoted in media and our surroundings. Embrace your uniqueness and remember that you are already enough!

Psalm 139:14

14 I will praise thee; for I am fearfully and wonderfully made: marvellous are thy works; and that my soul knoweth right well.

9. Weary Travelers

Running from chaos.

Nowhere to hide.

Looking for shelter.

Safety to abide.

All is so different.

The food, the dress

Nothing is easy.

A journey under duress

Hoping for smiles.

A stranger to become friend.

Do they know about my struggles?

Weariness from all these miles.

War, crime, poverty, and danger can provoke certain populations to flee their homeland. I cannot imagine how frightening and disheartening it could be to end up in an unfamiliar environment with no belongings or prospects.

Empathy and kindness are needed in this refugee crisis.

Leviticus 19:34

34 But the stranger that dwelleth with you shall be unto you as one born among you, and thou shalt love him as thyself; for ye were strangers in the land of Egypt: I am the Lord your God.

10. Strangers

A sea of people

Who can I trust?

Walking by them every day

Averting eyes seems like a must.

By chance, do we have something in common?

Similar hobbies - life goals to achieve.

Families to raise.

Reasons to believe.

Our hearts all beat the same.

Blood flows and revives

My fear of these "strangers"

Is something to tame?

At your school, workplace, church, or other social gathering have you ever taken the time to notice a new face that may look shy and alone? I consider it a joy to welcome these new people and try to make them feel included.

How about you?

Hebrews 13:1-2

13 Let brotherly love continue.

2 Be not forgetful to entertain strangers: for thereby some have entertained angels unawares.

11. Limitations

Many visits to my doctor.

My illness requires frequent care.

Most days I'm at home.

With not much to do.

Sometimes feeling useless

Wishing to experience something new.

Stay home I'm told.

Better to be safe.

Take care not to exert.

Dare not to be bold.

Must I live life subdued?

Or can I learn a new skill?

Maybe I'll try this time.

My dream to fulfill.

Sometimes those with a medical and or mental health diagnosis may feel like they are stuck in a box of limitations.

I like the term neural plasticity that describes that our brain is always regenerating new circuits and pathways, especially when we try and learn new things.

No matter what labels you may feel have been stamped across your life, I pray that you will continue to learn and contribute with your own unique abilities.

Philippians 4:13

13 I can do all things through Christ which strengtheneth me.

12. Unique

My difference makes me awkward.

Everyone else gets the award

Can't really help it – I was born this way.

Sometimes not chosen – left pondering dismay.

But yes, myself, I need to remind.

I can always improve.

Even advance my state of mind.

Hone a unique skill.

Enroll in a new class

Get a jumpstart on joy.

Enrich my life will.

I urge you to break out of your boxes. Try new things. Read, learn, grow.

It's never too late!

1 John 5:4

4 For whatsoever is born of God overcometh the world: and this is the victory that overcometh the world, even our faith.

13. Touch

Just a common handshake.

Eyes of sincere gaze.

This touch of another.

Can make it or break

Elevate my mood.

Even my life up to raise.

A hug brings delight.

Calms my human fright.

Like a kiss on the lips

Can smooth out life's dips.

Compassionate caring, and interest in others is welcome on this sometimes arduous life journey. We can help someone overcome life hurdles, and have the strength to go on with our personalized actions of love.

Proverbs 24:26

26 Every man shall kiss his lips that giveth a right answer.

14. Windows

Sustain our embrace.

Your eyes locked on mine.

No matter the color or even the race.

Calms all the noise.

Suspends frantic time.

Deep into my soul.

The windows are bare.

When you gaze into my eyes.

Out goes my care.

Taking the quiet time to listen with sincere eye contact is like a soothing balm in the midst of life chaos and introspection. No one is immune to this beautiful healing of individual attention.

Matthew 6:22

22 The light of the body is the eye: if therefore thine eye be single, thy whole body shall be full of light.

15. Nature Love

Green grass tickles my feet.

Rays of the sun

Warms me with heat.

Sweet animals smiling.

Likens all of us as one.

Waves of the sea

kissing the shore.

Perfect in beauty.

Fling wide the door.

Gentle caress of fall's crisp air.

Leaves flying down.

Blurring yellow – orange.

Not even a care.

Forest bathing denotes healing for a weary soul. Trees, sunshine, fresh air, or watching still waters are soothing medicine to quiet our senses, and bring refreshment to our nervous system. Clarity of mind along with soul-searching can be a much needed reward. We can turn off the external, shut down the noise, and relax in the presence of our Almighty Creator.

Isaiah 55:12

12 For ye shall go out with joy, and be led forth with peace: the mountains and the hills shall break forth before you into singing, and all the trees of the field shall clap their hands.

16. Exotic Adventure

Travels abroad.

New places to go.

Spices to taste

Go with the flow.

Ticket for the plane

Or all aboard a train?

Perhaps a voyage at sea

Just let loose and be free.

Customs, cultures, ideas to find.

Let down your hair.

Relax and unwind.

Where have you already traveled to? And where else would you love to visit? Getting out of our daily routines and exploring new adventures can breathe fresh life into our perspectives and insights.

Psalm 16:11

11 Thou wilt shew me the path of life: in thy presence is fulness of joy; at thy right hand there are pleasures for evermore.

17. Family Time

Back-and-forth – pushing the swing.

Enjoying my kids – hearing them sing.

Watching their games.

Cheering them on.

Unpacking the snacks.

Out on the lawn.

Helping with chores.

Getting it done.

Succeeding in life.

Opening new doors.

Sometimes life can feel like a treadmill of work, chores, and endless obligations. Choosing downtime alone, and with our families will yield bountiful rewards and blessings for all.

Proverbs 22:6

6 Train up a child in the way he should go:

and when he is old, he will not depart from it.

18. Notice Me

Does anyone see?

Can they even relate?

Sometimes invisible

Wondering if they hate.

Which shoes to wear?

Just to fit in

What style for my hair?

Just hoping to win.

Does anyone see?

Can they even relate?

Sometimes invisible.

Wondering if they hate.

Must I jump through the hoops?

Trying to impress.

Rearrange my likes.

Even the style of my dress.

Does anyone see?

Can they even relate?

Sometimes invisible

Wondering if they hate.

Thank you, my friend

For providing a chance.

Including me in

on this exciting life dance!

People of all ages can sometimes feel starved for attention, eye contact, and conversation. As we go about our day, it can be a mutual enriching experience to notice each other, and inquire about each others well-being.

1 Thessalonians 5:11

11 Wherefore comfort yourselves together, and edify one another, even as also ye do.

19. Kindness

Just takes a moment to be kind.

Speak to the heart and also to the mind.

Maybe just a smile is all that they need

Without having to beg or even to plead.

When you brighten someone's road

blessings for both will explode.

Rich treasures are free.

For me, he, and she.

You have this gift already within

Don't keep it locked up, safe in a bin.

Unlock the key

and let it fly free,

Let it spill - it won't make a mess.

Only to gladden, and ultimately to bless!

Kindness is a precious commodity in our hectic paced routines. Sometimes it can make or break whether we feel stressed or a sense of calmness and peace.

Ephesians 4:32

32 And be ye kind one to another, tenderhearted, forgiving one another, even as God for Christ's sake hath forgiven you.

20. Generosity

What gifts will you give with others to share?

Your time, your attention

These things show that you care.

A helping hand.

Burdens to bear.

We're all brothers and sisters.

Even when life is unfair.

So break open your bank.

Untap your reserve.

Shower onto others.

And fill up their tank.

Pay it forward they say.

Just to brighten someone's day

The secret they don't tell.

Is that it will also fill up your own life well!

Giving to others is a quick mood elevator for both parties. What a sense of joy we feel to give our time or a carefully picked out gift. And the added bonus of seeing a smile on someone's face is like icing on the cake.

Proverbs 22:9

9 He that hath a bountiful eye shall be blessed; for he giveth of his bread to the poor.

21. Friends

You are enough.

A true beauty to share.

You bring to the table

A smorgasbord of flair.

Don't hide who is you.

Let it shine – let it glow.

Release all your gifts

Like a river they flow.

You are enough.

So blessed to finally meet.

Made your acquaintance.

Makes my life even sweet.

Friendships can be cultivated in every type of situation. Humility, kindness, smiles, and a generous spirit can light the way.

Proverbs 17:17

17 A friend loveth at all times, and a brother is born for adversity.

22. Your Turn

Now it's your turn.

I hand you the pen.

Stir up your gifts.

Mix it up – make it churn.

We need your unique voice.

In this world full of choice

So come on – let it out.

Release the creative - along with a shout!

Show us what's inside

No need to look down.

Head up - stand straight

Your talent – your pride!

I am extremely ready to see now what you will create. It could be poetry, art, stories, comedy, spoken, word, etc., etc....

Get creative!

2 Timothy 1

6 Wherefore I put thee in remembrance that thou stir up the gift of God, which is in thee by the putting on of my hands.

7 For God hath not given us the spirit of fear; but of power, and of love, and of a sound mind.

Thanks for hanging out and enjoying this poetry devotional! Please share this with others.

For more inspirational wellness and CrEaTiVe Entertainment with a purpose see you at

NURSEANNE.COM

More exciting and soul-enriching titles by Nurse Anne:

Mental Healing
Poetry Devotional

Inviting you to investigate and embrace God's promise of power, love, and a sound mind.

By Nurse Anne

Presenting my original spoken word pieces in this devotional.

Life challenges are discussed, along with God-ordained courage and healing to help us turn away from mindsets controlled by fear. Inspiration to step into our true destiny of a faith walk and purpose-driven path.

Inspiration

Battles

Devotional

By Nurse Anne

Biblical Medicine for Real Life

Biblical Medicine for Real Life. Soul-searching with a dose of encouragement!

The battle to stay inspired can seem overwhelming at times. Yet, God reminds us that our faith should not be in the power of people but in His wisdom. Fear not, as you embark on this journey of allowing the Lord to search your life. Let the Holy Spirit's spotlight penetrate your heart, mind, will, emotions, your everything. Whatever might seem difficult for the moment will yield a reward of peace and purpose.

Find new hope and inspiration on this A to Z devotional exploration.

WORD

PUzZLeS

Devotional

Wisdom and Biblical Rx inspired by the Ultimate Wordsmith.

By Nurse Anne

Interesting words linked to everyday life drama, & our inner thought struggles, then paired with relevant Biblical prescriptions. Get your dose. Overcome and thrive.

WORD PUzZLeS A-Z

From Nurseanne.com

Ministry to Inspire, Advocate, Encourage, Create.

Certified Emergency and Mental Health RN.

Encouragement, hope, and new light for your life journey. Unique words along with inspirational wellness and Biblical prescriptions. Medicine for your soul.

Energized Health

Body, Mind and Spirit

Lifestyle Devotional

By Nurse Anne

Inspirational Wellness along with Biblical prescriptions to develop a mind at peace and to cultivate your walk with God. Also, health tips designed to jumpstart your energized life of purpose.

Nurse Anne is a certified emergency and mental health registered nurse of 30 years and still going. Enjoy this devotional designed to propel your total health for body, mind, & spirit.

Let's get started!

The Mental Files

First 6 Stories Edition

--- Sheep Among Wolves

--- Dr. John Doe

--- A Tent Under the Bridge

--- Defenders of the Weak

--- Ready, Willing and Able

--- Out Of Control

By Nurse Anne

Also now available as an *Exciting Audiobook!!*

Audible and iTunes

Ride along with the frontline workers as they try to rescue those in crisis. Mental, physical and spiritual. Thought and memory disorders, disabilities, homelessness, addictions, despair, bullying, and more inspiration battles. Not to mention the inner thought strongholds and relationship drama of the workers.

What role does God play in the outcome?

The shifts are 24/7. Buckle up for the compelling drama series filled with danger, action, suspense, romance, faith and inspiration.

The Mental Files:

Book 1: Sheep Among Wolves - intro

Ride along with officer Leon and caseworker Lita as they try to convince the man hovered on the edge of the bridge not to do the unthinkable?

And will the naive young lady with the unexpected test result whose mind is being ravaged by frightening hallucinations trust the frontline workers? Or will she listen to her so-called boyfriend that she met at the bus stop? If only the little lamb knew the dangerous plans the street predator had in mind for her.

Will the lonely caseworker fall for the handsome officer in spite of the nagging red flags? Will she rely on her faith or go with her feelings?

Will the young man caught in the web of crime find a way out?

Ride along on the journey as the drama continues in the next story.

The Mental Files: Dr. John Doe

Why was the gray-haired man with a confused look running in and out of traffic screaming that he was a doctor? Follow Officer Leon, caseworker Lita, the nurses, and their newest ride along on the adventure from the street to the healthcare system. Can they figure out who the mystery man really is? And what about the young man who just narrowly escaped a life of crime? Will his negative thoughts pull him down further and place his loved ones in danger? Or can he find inspiration to pursue a better life?

Will the caseworker and officer take their relationship to the next level? Thought battles and memory struggles rage in this ongoing drama.

Continue the adventure in the next story.

The Mental Files: A Tent Under The Bridge

Why does Abigail continue to live under the bridge? Will she allow the frontline workers to help her find a safer and healthier life? Will her long-lost mystery daughter be able to forgive her? Or will Abigail's choices place her daughter in further danger?

Ride along with Mars on his first paramedic shifts. Can he handle the intense trauma and drama?

Will the handsome officer ask his big question to the beautiful caseworker? Or will his buddies convince him he will never change and would be making a mistake?

Join the frontline workers as they continue rescue efforts for the minds and lives of the vulnerable.

The story continues.

The Mental Files: Defenders of the Weak

Can Chandra break out of her paralyzing fear and anxiety? Stop allowing the bullies to take over her existence and place her in danger? Will she be able to help the stranger with a similar struggle? Or will the opposition take them both down?

Will the frontline worker's project to help the less fortunate be thwarted by the community and church members who don't want their comfort disturbed?

Is the opposition willing to place others in danger to keep their status quo?

Strongholds to be broken. A God who is able.

The shifts are 24/7. Buckle up as the bumpy ride continues.

The Mental Files: Ready, Willing, and Able

Ride along with the frontline workers on the continuing drama as they discover that problems exist in every type of household. For richer or poorer. And sometimes, the unlikeliest of people can be the actual heroes. Abilities triumph over a spectrum of doubt.

Will the young paramedic make wise or hasty relationship decisions? Why does the mental health nurse get sent to the ER? Can the community and church finally accept the so-called different people in their midst?

Leading you into the action with the season finale.

The Mental Files: Out Of Control

Season Finale

One more won't hurt. When does the seemingly harmless fun cross into the realm of out of control? Placing others in danger.

Does the entitled patient comply with his treatment? Or will he make the frontline workers pay?

Will the big event get canceled due to the officer's mistake? Can he be forgiven? Given the benefit of the doubt?

What will reign? New beginnings or old habits?

Get ready to be a part of the adventure, advocacy, awareness, and action!

For more Inspirational

Wellness and

CrEaTiVe Entertainment

With a Purpose see you at

NURSEANNE.COM

Be Blessed

Made in the USA
Middletown, DE
06 September 2023

37860164R10060